Table of Contents

Introduction

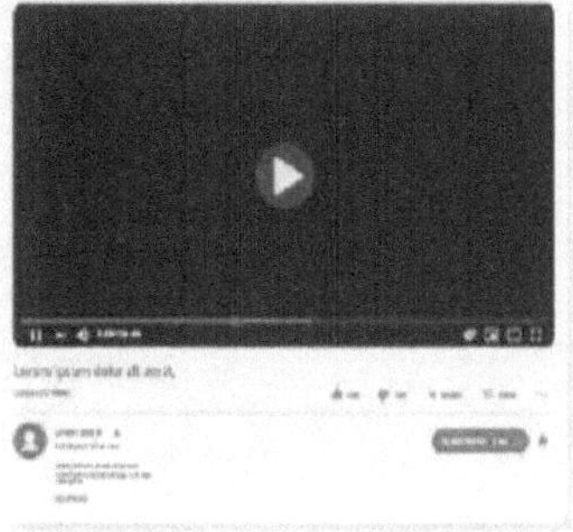

The world has truly become digital and it has made content easily available. But with the wide availability of content, it also made people's attention spans shorter. And the breadth of content means multiple forms of it are all competing for your limited attention. Why not provide the best possible content? And videos are now emerging as the content of choice. And this is what we will be exploring through YouTube and YouTube Channels.

In a study to determine which fares better in terms of engagement in social media, researchers found video to do better than images. This should not be a surprise because of the fact that video stimulates the brain better than any other media. Below is a comparison of the brain stimulation that video offers vs. that of images and text:

Video	Image	Text
Simulates the Following	Simulates the Following	Simulates the Following
Visual Senses - yes	Visual Senses - yes	Visual Senses - not that match
Authority Senses - yes	Authority Senses - no	Authority Senses - no
Kinesthic Senses - yes	Kinesthic Senses - no	Kinesthic Senses - no

With the comparison you can already see a clear winner. The video format trumps all the others because it appeals to the needs of the brain. First and foremost, the brain just hates to be bored. And while images can be powerful, it's not as powerful as a truly engaging piece of video. If you find this hard to believe then check out the data below on the top 2 social media platforms that has the most number of users:

The common denominator with both platforms is their ability to post, store, and share videos. While Facebook has a more complex structure, YouTube's platform is very simple—it allows its users to upload videos and share them. It's as simple as that. That's why everyone is turning to YouTube for everything, whether it's a tutorial for a DIY project, a musical performance from their favorite musical group to just watching cute cats do cute things on video.

And that power to captivate an audience's attention through videos is magnified to a staggering degree when you curate your content and create a YouTube Channel. By creating a channel, it becomes easier for you to reach your target audience as you streamline your well-thought-out content. In fact, YouTube Channels have become ubiquitous strategies in marketing that even big-name products have their own channels. And it's not only for the big boys, Vloggers and influencers are sharing their content through YouTube and earning six figures (or more) from it.

As you read further you will learn how to set up your own YouTube Channel. Not only that, but you will also learn how to create and curate your content so that it sends a powerful message to your target audience. This way, your videos (through your YouTube Channel) will gain traction and have the widest possible reach. And of course, all these will not be possible without a good content plan. The creation of that plan will also be discussed in the Chapter 4.

It doesn't matter if you're doing this as part of your product's branding strategy or you just want to express yourself, Creating a YouTube Channel is definitely a big plus. With an official channel, you or your brand can have a public presence. Aside from that, here are other reasons why it's advantageous to have a YouTube Channel:

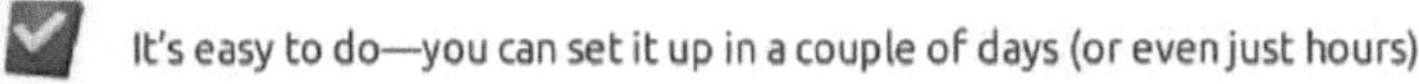
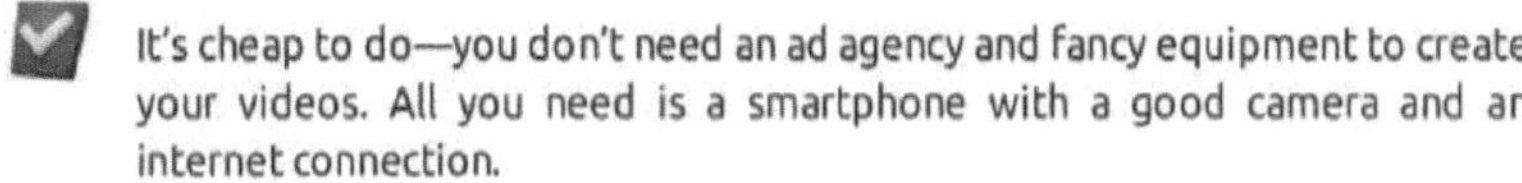

- It's easy to do—you can set it up in a couple of days (or even just hours).

- It's cheap to do—you don't need an ad agency and fancy equipment to create your videos. All you need is a smartphone with a good camera and an internet connection.

- It has a wide reach—you can reach a wider audience with YouTube's 2 billion users and subscribers.

- It can be linked—your content can all be brought together because everything is linkable. You can link your Youtube Channel with your Social Media and Web Page. At the same time, you can also link your Social Media and Web Page in your YouTube Channel.

- It can help you rank higher in web searches—since YouTube is integrated with Google's Universal Search algorithm, it will be easier for users to find you or your product if you have a YouTube Channel. More of this will be discussed in the Chapter 3 or optimizing your YouTube Channel.

- You can earn if you run AdSense—AdSense is Google's way to advertise and, in turn, will earn money for the Channel hosting the ad. By running AdSense, your Channel not only reaches a certain target market but also earns through your users' views and clicks.

And without further ado, let's get on with it and start learning how we can set up our own YouTube Channel.

Chapter 1
Creating Your YouTube Channel

First things first, you have to have the following so that you can go ahead and create your YouTube Channel:

A

Google Account

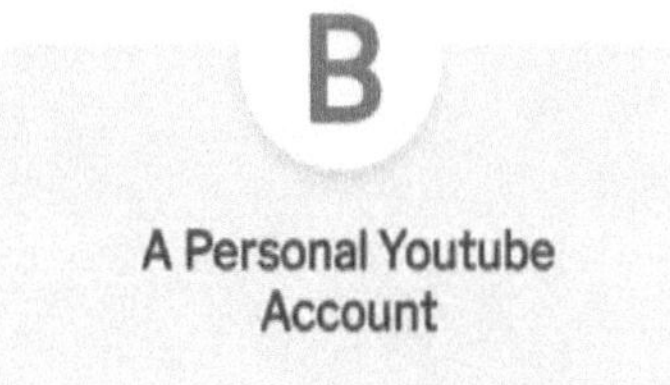

B

A Personal Youtube Account

Once you have those then you can begin. Log in to your YouTube account, click the profile button on the upper right of the screen and you should see a 'Create a Channel' option appear.

Now you have the option to either use your name or to create a custom name using a brand account. So let's create a brand account.

Next, you will have to create Your Channel Name

Choose one that's relevant to your brand.
Remember to choose wisely because this will
have a future impact on your brand's reputation
and how your users will search your content.
Once you have chosen a brand name, type it on
the Add Channel Name box and click Create.

Create your channel name

You can use your brand's name or another name. A good channel name represents
you and your content. You can change your channel name at any time

Channel name

Add channel name

☐ I understand that I am creating a new Google Account with its own settings,
including YouTube search and watch history. Learn more

CANCEL   CREATE

Next, you will be asked to upload a Profile Picture. Though not necessary (you can skip
this part) but you need a picture that will tie you up with your brand. You can choose to
upload a logo of your brand or a headshot of you (if you are marketing yourself). After
uploading your profile picture you will be asked to write a channel description. Do this
so that your users will have an idea of what your channel is about. This will also make it
easier to search for your content later. Lastly, you will be asked to add links to your
other platforms: your Website, Facebook, Instagram, and Twitter. This step is important
and will be discussed further in Chapter 5.

Congratulations, you have now created your YouTube Channel. But you are not done
yet. You have to continue customizing your channel to make it more effective. Next on
the to-do list is to add Channel Art. The Channel Art feature of your YouTube Channel
lets you further personalize your channel. In keeping with your branding, you want your
channel art to give a good representation of what you (or your brand) are about.

As you click on the Customize Channel button,

you will be led to YouTube's blank template. Click it and a pop-up window will appear where you can upload a photo to serve as your banner. After that, it's all about cropping the photo to make it a banner. Make sure to choose a landscape photo with areas ideal for cropping. Ideal size for photos to upload as channel art would be 2560 pixels (width) x 1440 pixels (height). Do note that there is a minimum size for your uploads—2048 x 1152. Anything smaller and YouTube will tell you to find a bigger sized picture. Click 'Select' once you're satisfied with your uploaded image.

Before we go shooting vids, one last thing your channel art will require is your icon. You can find it at the upper left-hand side of the channel art template (it's usually designated with the first letter of the name you registered the account to). Click the icon with the letter and upload another image. For the icon image, feel free to upload your brand's logo or any other picture that best represents you or your brand. Once you upload an image then your channel is all set.

Now let's get started with making video content. This is what our YouTube Channel is all about.

Chapter 2:

CREATING AND UPLOADING VIDEOS

Shooting Your Video

What's a channel without any video? So let's go make one. But first, you need to have the proper equipment. Even if you don't have the money to buy the equipment, you can always use your ingenuity. You can start with repurposed DIY equipment as you start and once you make money you can buy equipment that the professionals use.

Here's what you will need for a start:

- A Smartphone with a Camera
- Something to hold your phone
- A Light Source
- A plain Background

If you have all four

(and you should have these at home) then you're all set to shoot your video. But for further understanding, below is a detailed step by step guide on how to shoot on the cheap:

 **Prepare your smartphone** and set the camera to shoot on video at the highest resolution and a decent frame per second rate. To get the best possible output, set your videos at 1080p (this is the resolution for HDTV) and at least 30 frames per second. For action shots (where the subject moves a lot), set it at 60 frames per second.

 **Check the lens of the camera** for smudges (as this is bound to happen). Clean with a microfiber cloth if needed. You don't want to end up with a high-resolution blur.

 **Install a plain background** as a backdrop. A simple clean wall with a solid color will do. Of you can put up a plain cloth (like a blanket) on the wall. You want to make the background as simple as possible because you want your foreground (your subject) to stand-out.

 **Set up a light source** to augment your indoor light, especially if you're shooting at night. Most indoor lighting fixtures are situated overhead. Overhead lighting makes the subject look unflattering on camera. Plus they create shadows, which may become distracting. The simplest way to do this is to set up a lamp on the floor just a little bit in front of the camera but out of view on the viewfinder.

If there's ample natural light from outside then it's also advisable to use that light. All you have to do is open the window and situate your camera near it. Natural light always looks flattering and will bring out great colors on the video.

5   **Next, prop up** the tool to hold the camera. Most people will use a tripod for this. But even without a tripod, you can still fashion something that will do the job. Place objects on a small table, such as books, that will hold the camera steady and in place as you shoot your video. This helps when you don't have a buddy who will hold up the camera for you. Plus, hands that hold cameras tend to get shaky. So prop up that cam (tripods are still the best option here). Don't forget to shoot in landscape mode. This will make your video easily viewable in all devices.

6   **Connecting a microphone** will greatly help but is not necessary. Your phone's built-in mic should be enough to do the job. What an external mic does is it directs its focus on the sound source and filter out the ambient noise. If you don't have an external microphone, make sure that the source of sound is close to the microphone of your phone. You will capture some background noise but that should be fine as long as the foreground sound is clear and highly audible.

There you have it. By doing those steps you should be able to produce your very own video. For sure, it will not take you too much time to do it. And you didn't even have to spend a dime because all the equipment you need can be found right in your home.

Uploading your First Video—
the Channel Trailer

So armed with the knowledge of shooting a video, why don't you shoot your very first one for your YouTube Channel. You can reach out more to your target audience if you have a short trailer video telling them what your channel is about. Here's how you can upload a trailer video on your YouTube Channel:

1   Shoot a short video following the steps above. Don't worry, you don't need to edit this for now since this will only be about 2 minutes of footage.

2   Upload the video to your YouTube account. Then go to your Channel and select 'Customize Channel'.

3   Find the Home button and head on to the 'For the New Visitors' button and click it.

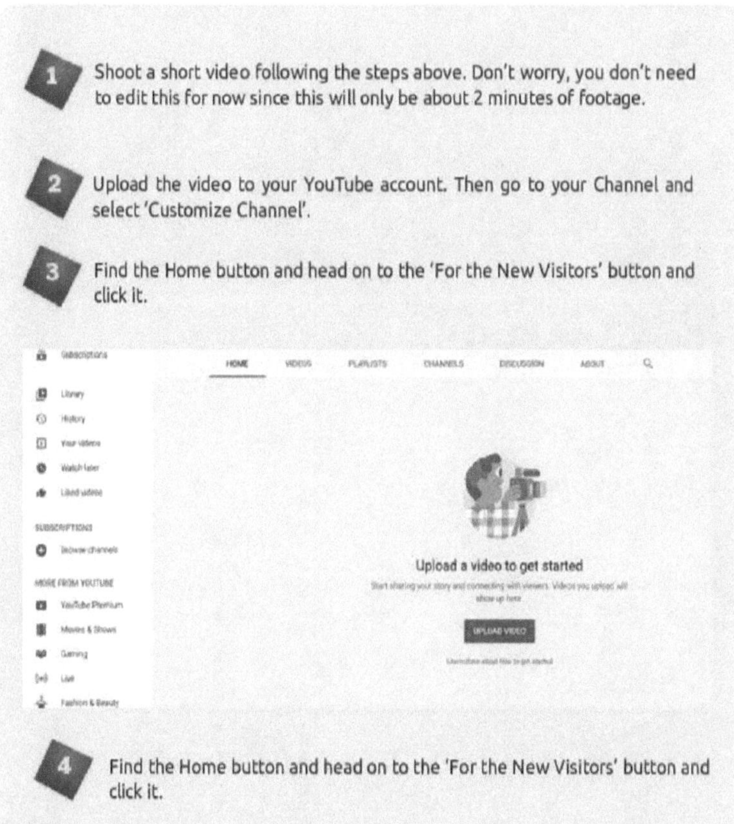

4   Find the Home button and head on to the 'For the New Visitors' button and click it.

Voila! You have shot your first video and uploaded a Channel Trailer all in one go.

Editing Videos

As you shoot more vides you will come to realize that raw footage simply will not cut it. You need to do post-production to spruce up your videos. So here's a simple guide on how to edit your videos to make them stand out:

 Don't be afraid to try it out. There are plenty of online video editing tools out there (some of them are even free). Here's a list of the video editing tools you can use:

https://filmora.wondershare.com/video-editor/free-online-video-editor.html

 Make your videos short so that it's easier and faster to edit. Your hardware will also thank you for it. Video editing software eats up a lot of your processor's memory. So the longer the video the more stressed your processor will be. The more stressed out your processor, the longer it will take you to edit.

1. Cut out the unnecessary parts. This is what video editing is for—you get to extract footage that should not have been there in the first place. There will be instances where you make some mistakes with your lines or a certain shot was ruined by an unwanted photobomber appearing in the background. You can cut these out, Make judicious use of this function so that your video flows well and transitions seamlessly from one scene to the next.

2. Use the effects functions but not too gratuitously. The video editing software will have a host of effects in store for you to play around with. Feel free to let your creativity fly but do not overdo it. Simplicity is still an understated feature when it comes to making videos. For a start, you can do the basic text effects to make the content more easily understandable for the viewer.

2. Use music to enhance your video and place them strategically. A good strategy for using music in videos is in the opening and closing sequences. Additionally, you might want to also include some background music in your video to liven it up. Again, be judicious in your choice of music and where you put them.

What you will notice is that all these "technical" aspects of video making have been demystified. All it takes is just some effort at researching and experimenting and you can easily become a videographer.

You didn't need to go to school for this knowledge. This is the beauty of technology—it has become democratized. Anyone can do it now. And since anyone can do it easily, you have to do your best to create content that is unique so that it will stand out from the rest.

Chapter 3:

OPTIMIZING YOUR YOUTUBE CHANNEL

Optimizing Your Channel

Optimizing your YouTube Channel means you're making it easy for your target audience to find you. Understand that everything that happens now happens online. So if your target audience is looking for you (or they may be looking for a certain product or service that you offer) they will most likely search for you using a search engine

And YouTube is not only a video sharing site; it's also a search engine on its own. In fact, YouTube is second only to Google in terms of search functionality. And do you know who owns YouTube? That's right; it's Google. Their Universal Search functionality feeds off of each other. So if you're easily searchable on YouTube, you should be easily searchable as well in Google (and vice versa).

So how do we make our YouTube Channel optimized? Below are some steps that can help in optimization:

 Make sure to fill out the 'About' Section of your Channel. You should have received this prompt when you created your channel. Make sure that all details about you, your brand, and the channel are there. The description you place in the About Section will appear in other places on your YouTube Channel so this piece of text information is vital when users want to know more about you.

 When you upload videos you will notice that you will be asked to come up with a title and some description of the video. The title and description will be vital when your user has finally chanced upon your video by searching for it either on YouTube or using a search engine. It is through the title and description that your target audience will know if they found the right video.

Lastly, you will also be asked to come up with tags. This is the most important piece of the optimization puzzle. Tags are keywords or key phrases that a search engine uses to easily identify what it is looking for.

Think of yourself going to the grocery store looking for a certain item. If the store does not have tags on their products then you would not know what those products are. But with tags, you will easily identify what those items are and whether you want to buy them or not.

That's what tags do to your videos. And the great thing about them is that you can have multiple tags in your videos. The more tags (and quality ones where the keywords and phrases are relevant) then the easier for your videos to rank higher in the search results.

How to Come Up with Great Tags

Remember that coming up with tags for your videos is not just a random thing where you put down whatever it was on your mind at the time of uploading. Careful consideration should be made when thinking about what tags to use for your videos. Below are some tips for you to come up with great tags what will help your videos rank better:

 When thinking of tags for videos, think of the following: theme, topic, category, and niche. Form these, think of what keywords or phrases come to mind. These words will be what you will be using as your tags.

 For the specific video's first tag, come up with the exact keyword or key phrase you want to rank for. As an example, if your video is about cats doing cute stuff then you want your key phrase to be 'cute cats video' because this will be the most likely phrase users will input in their search engines. By having that tag, your video will be one of those that will appear when that specific key phrase is typed.

 To improve rankings, other tags must be placed to include both broad and specific scopes. By doing this you will leave nothing to chance. When going broad with our example in number 2, you might want to include the tag 'cute animals'. This way, your cute cat video will still be included in the search results even if it was a search on cute animals. And by going specific, you might want to name your tag as 'cute Persian cats'. This way, the more specific searches will still yield your cat video.

 Another good strategy is to have tail words to go after your first tag. Tail words are suggested words the search engine will give as you type keywords. Using the example of cute cats, when you type those words you will see suggested tail words with it like: 'cute cats sleeping' or 'cute cats playing'. You might want to add those tail words as one of your tags.

5. Don't over-tag. It's not a numbers game when it comes to coming up with a tag for your videos. Too many tags will also confuse search engines and will actually harm the ranking of your videos. A good number of tags to aim for is at 8. You can have a lesser number of tags but more than 8 tags is really a lot (and most of them might be redundant).

6. Tagging is about keywords and phrases—as such don't put in too many words. You're not writing a story so make your tags brief. The shorter the tag the easier it is to be searchable. But as you make your tags short, don't sacrifice quality words in the process. The number of words to aim for when coming up with a tag is 1. But you can go as high as 3 or 4. Anything more than that is a sentence (and not a tag).

7. You can also copy tags from similar videos. Search up a video, preferably a popular one, and see what tags they are using. To help you out, here's a free tool you can use to see tags used by videos: www.tubebuddy.com.

8. Lastly, you can let the internet do the work for you. There are online tools that will help you with coming up with good tags for your videos like www.TagsYouTube.com. All you have to do is to type a keyword and it will throw out other suggested tags for you.

Optimizing is your best bet in order for your videos to become easily searchable. There's a saying that goes: "Build it and they will come". But for the digital age, we need to update that saying to: "Build it, optimize it, and they will come". The digital world is now too crowded with content. If you don't optimize, your videos might end up lost in a sea of videos. Optimization is what separates the viral YouTube channels from the also-rans. Take the time to learn about it and see your subscriber count soar.

Chapter 4:

CREATING A CONTENT PLAN

Coming Up with Content

Now that we have the technical background covered, let's move on to the creative side of making videos for our channel. Coming up with great content requires a great plan first and foremost. When you look at all those great channels, the content didn't just suddenly pop up in the heads of the creators. It took careful planning and implementation. So how do you go about coming up with a great content plan? First, you have to consider what kind of videos (content) you want to put out on your channel. Below are some suggested content you can use:

1. **_Tutorials_ and How-To Guides**—these videos are usually informational step-by-step guides on how to do certain skills or activities. People nowadays will search the internet (and especially YouTube) to learn how to do things. These things may be DIY carpentry projects, art stuff, or even how to complete video game levels (called walkthroughs).

If you know how to do something, you can surely put up a video of you doing it. All you have to do is to show your audience how it's done while enumerating the steps. A discussion per step might also be helpful.

2. **Vlogs (or A Day in the Life Of)**—the beauty of the democratized access to the internet is that it becomes a great equalizer. Now, anyone can access and post whatever they want on the internet. Whereas in the past only the big media companies can churn out videos, now any regular Joe can do so. Enter Vlogs.

Vlogs are video blogs. They are about nothing and everything at the same time. They are usually videos of what a typical day is like for the Channel owner. Think of them as a journal or diary but in video format. And unlike a diary where you keep it secret, the Vlogger is putting out the video in public (on YouTube for that matter) for everyone to see. Looking at a Vlog typically puts you in the eyes of an interested observer of someone who lives in a bubble. This fact excites a lot of people and has led to the rise of Vloggers becoming influencers.

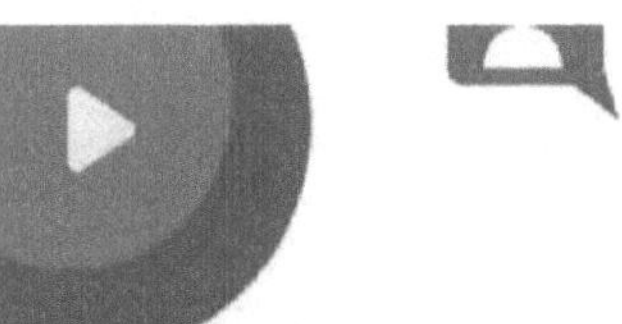

Product or Service Reviews—these videos are typically helpful for would-be buyers so that they don't experience buyer's remorse. People are turning to the internet to seek out reviews of products and services to help them make the decision. By doing a product review, you let your viewers know more about the product and whether it is a good buy or not.

Product or service review videos feature the product (or service) and will have you as the reviewer. The reviewer will go through the features of the product and will assess whether the product is worth the money that they paid for it. You would also typically find these reviews pitting one product against another. If a certain YouTube Channel has garnered a huge subscriber base, companies will be the ones knocking on the channel owner's door to have their products reviewed. Some companies will even pay or give freebies to the channel owner. These freebies can also be made into "Unboxing" videos where the reviewer opens the box that the product came in as a sort of a ritual before doing the product review.

Funny Memes or Comedic Sketches—there are people born with the gift of comedy and they are more than happy to share that gift through videos. These may come in the form of skits where the footage is staged or it may be a spontaneous video of a funny moment happening.

The great thing about these videos is that they are the ones shared the most on social media. People love to laugh and they love it even more if the ones they laugh at are people they can relate to. And it is a given fact that people will go to YouTube just to browse funny videos. If you have comedic talent, then these types of videos will be the bomb.

5. Education or
Training Videos

These videos deliver a theory or a concept and explain it to the viewing audience. Unlike the tutorial or how-to guide videos, education or training videos do not show the practical application of a skill. These videos are knowledge-based and more often than not just involves a lecture on the concepts.

You can practically search for any theory and concept and there should be an educational explainer video about it. If you have a particular expertise in a given field then you should definitely let your audience learn more about it. It doesn't have to be boring—check out the TED talks and see how to successfully do a lecture while keeping your audience's attention in check.

6.

Virtual Tour

These videos take the viewers to fun and exotic places without having to leave their homes. Makers of these videos go to these fun locations and shoot themselves giving a tour of the place. This way, the viewers get to see the place and learn a little bit more about its history and maybe some local trivia.

These virtual tour videos are also called Travelogues and will appeal to travel enthusiasts. As air travel becomes cheaper, people turn to these travelogues to find out more about certain travel destinations before they finally decide where to travel to. Or for those who simply can't afford to travel, virtual tour videos will make them experience the place through the eyes of the channel owner even without having to physically go to the place.

Performance Videos (Singing or Dancing)—people love to show off their dancing or singing prowess, even if they're not any good at it. But if you're particularly adept at singing or dancing (or both), then a video of your performance might be your ticket to stardom (Justin Bieber was discovered through YouTube).

These performance videos showcase your talent to the world. And it's just fun to perform in front of the camera. So sing your heart out and dance like there's no tomorrow. Shoot the performance on video and upload it on YouTube. If you're any good you should see an uptick in views. If you are exceptional, you just might get discovered. And it's not just for performance's sake, recording and performance artists are now turning to YouTube for marketing and branding.

Analyzing your Content

YouTube just upgraded its user interface to make it easier for their users to do analytics. Analytics will give the channel user information on what is happening with regards to the channel. The beauty of analytics is that it gives relevant data so that the channel owner will know what to do next. There are three things that analytics will tell you:

- Descriptive Data—basic data to give you a description of what is happening. On YouTube, examples of these data will be the number of views and the watch time.

- Prescriptive Data—advanced data and might be a combination of two or more data sets to tell the channel owner what to do next. For example, by comparing the number of views to watch times you might find that shorter videos have more watch times. This would tell you that you need to create shorter videos in the future.

- Descriptive Data—basic data to give you a description of what is happening. On YouTube, examples of these data will be the number of views and the watch time.

Your channel's dashboard will present a summary of your analytics for easy viewing. And if you click the 'Analytics' tab you will get more details and graphs of the analytics. Study the data so that you can come up with good descriptive data sets that will let you know what has been going on with your channel. You can then compare these data sets to come up with your Prescriptive Data. You can leave the hardcore Predictive Analytics to the professionals.

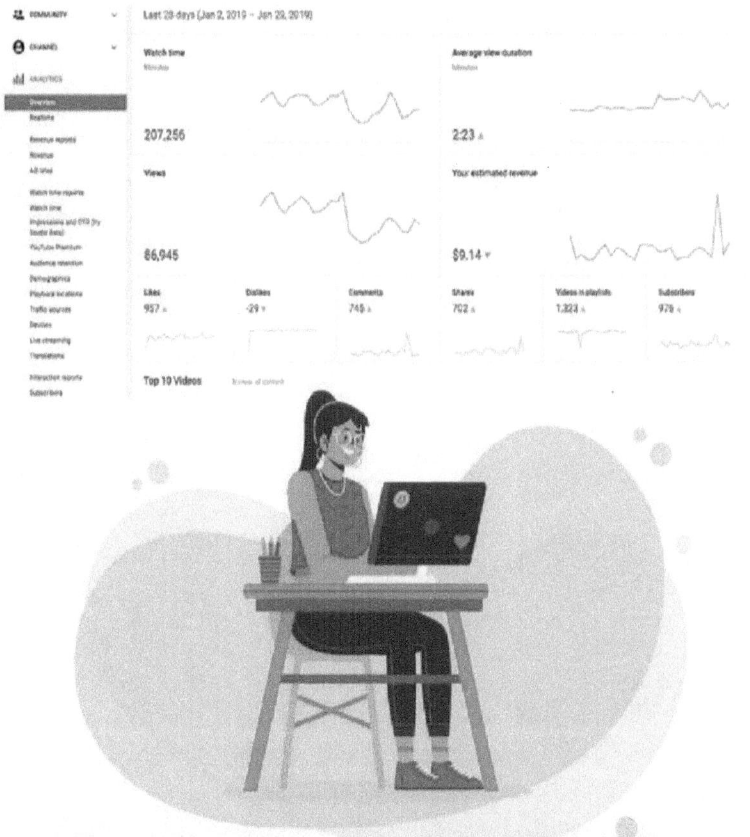

Chapter 5:

INTEGRATING YOUR CHANNEL
INTO YOUR OTHER

Online Platforms

When you Channel first created your channel you should have received a prompt to input links to your social media pages and your web page. If you skipped this part you can go back to it by going to your and clicking 'Customize Channel' and clicking the 'About' tab. You can fill out your links there as well as your email address.

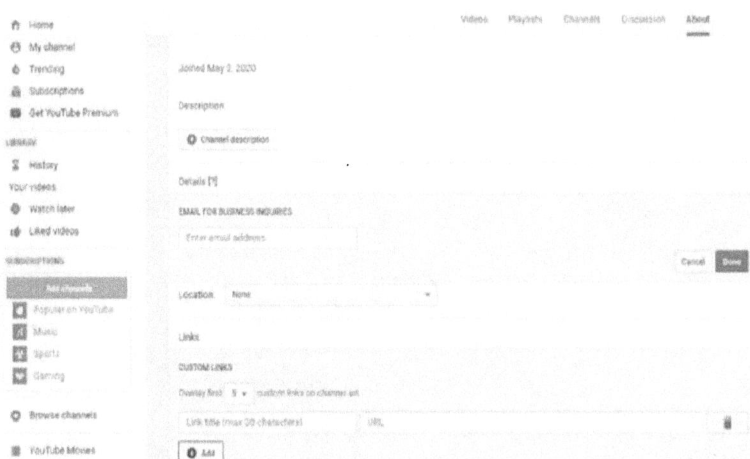

These links are important so that you can cross-market to your social media accounts. Your viewers will not want to just watch videos. They will also want to interact with you and your brand in different ways. Below are tips on how the different links from your Channel can enable you to interact with your subscribers in different ways:

Website—you need this link to show your viewers that you are a legit brand. After you succeed in getting the interest of your viewers they will want to find out more information about you. Your website is the best avenue for them to find out all this information. Further, your website should include your contact details. So should your viewer be interested in purchasing your product or availing your service, your website should be the one-stop-shop for interacting, contacting, and processing this transaction.

Facebook—this platform will get you a wider market reach because of its sheer number of users. The great thing about social media like Facebook is that you can get viral very fast because of its ability to share content. And even if it's not shared, your content will appear on your friends' feeds so there's a greater chance for discovery. Facebook has built a reputation as a wide social community of users who interact with each other. And one great feature is that YouTube videos can be shared as Facebook posts. You don't have to re-upload your videos from YouTube to Facebook. Just follow these steps:

https://smallbusiness.chron.com/embed-youtube-videos-facebook-pages-51118.html

3 **Instagram**—linking your channel to your Instagram account provides you with another venue to further extend your reach. Though Instagram has fewer users, it is a more closely-knit environment with a lot of interaction. And with Instagram, it's hard to create fake accounts so you know you're really interacting with a real person. This is why it has become the social media platform of choice for celebrities. If you're interacting with a known public figure on Instagram then you can be sure it's really them. So use your Instagram connections to drum up and funnel more organic views into your YouTube Channel.

Since Instagram is primarily a photo-sharing social media platform, you should come up with photo content to go along with your video. This can be your post on Instagram with an accompanying link to your YouTube Channel. Be creative in the images you post. Come up with photos that will give your target audience a better idea of your product and of yourself. This way, they will know that they are interacting with a real human being who is behind the brand.

4 **Twitter**—this platform is a great marketing tool because it limits your text posts to only 140 characters. Think of twitter as a way for you to write copy (a copy is a marketing term for information you want to send out for your product). But instead of a long winding piece, Twitter forces you to trim it down to make it more palatable to your audience. By doing so, the piece of information you put out is concise, direct to the point, and not at all boring. With the shortened attention spans of people these days, you definitely need something like Twitter.

Brands are using Twitter to not only send out information about the brand but also about upcoming events. Since it catches the attention of users easily, announcements and updates are regularly sent through Twitter. But it's not limited to just purely cold information sharing. Twitter is a great avenue to interact with your users and with other brands. In fact, many brands have become famous for engaging in Twitter wars with other brands. And they do it with just a play of words (limited to 140 characters).

And just like the other platforms, YouTube allows you to share the videos on your channel to Twitter. Here's a link on how to do it: https://www.magisto.com/blog/2019/03/18/how-to-post-videos-on-twitter-the-complete-guide/

5.
Other Social Media Accounts

you might have specialized social media accounts that you also want to include as links in your YouTube Channel. Do not limit yourself with the big 3. Know more about your brand and see if you can link it to a Social Media account that can zero-in further on your target market. You might want to consider the following social media platforms:

 **LinkedIn**	For professionals and job-seekers. If your channel content is geared towards professionals and career development then LinkedIn is a good platform to share your channel content
Pinterest	For hobby and craft enthusiasts. Your DIY projects, product reviews, and tutorials will certainly find a home in this social media platform
Behance	For serious artists, this platform is an avenue for them to share their work and create a portfolio
DeviantArt	Similar to Behance—a network where artists can share their work
Reddit	A community-based platform where users join topics of interest called sub-reddits. A lot of video content is shared on this platform.

So take advantage of what the online world has to offer. Link all your sites—social media and official website. These days, it doesn't take much to get your content out in the open. Most of the time it's for free and can be done with just a few clicks. You just have to harness the power of social media and create a bridge so that your content from one platform can cross to multiple other platforms. This is what makes content viral.

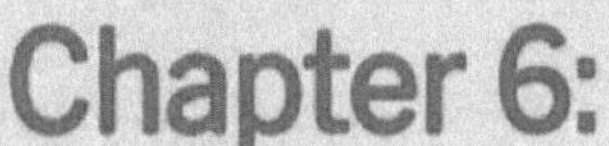

Chapter 6:

Engaging Your Subscribers

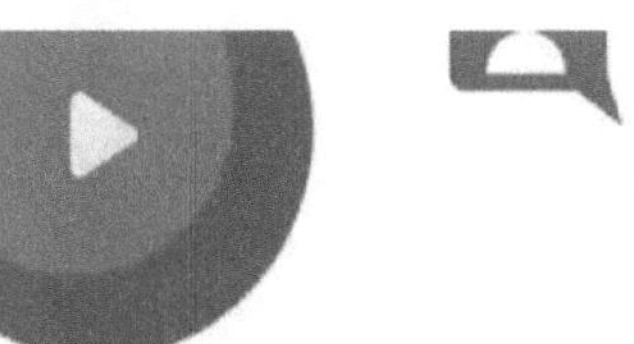

One advantage that YouTube has is that it has a comment capability. This means that anyone can leave a comment on your videos. This will leave plenty of room for interaction, whether you interact with your viewers and subscribers or they interact with each other. This feature makes YouTube a social media platform as well. You can get good feedback and insight on your brand through these interactions. Below are some tips on how to interact with those leaving comments on your videos and channel:

 Make it a habit of going through the comments section of your channel daily. See which comments you can learn from and which comments you can just ignore. There will be scathing remarks that might hurt but can actually point you towards a better direction on how you manage your content and your channel as a whole.

 Take time to thank those who made insightful and valuable comments—may they be positive or negative. In fact, you can take it a step further by creating a thank you video to show your appreciation to your subscribers (especially those who made the effort to leave a really insightful comment or two).

 Get conversations going between commenters by commenting back. They will appreciate the gesture and will keep on commenting (that's how conversations go after-all). By doing this you show to the community that there's breathing, thinking individual behind the brand that they can interact with.

 Get ideas on your next video from the suggestions in the comments. You not only get feedback on how you can improve but you also get great material for your upcoming content. Remember to acknowledge and thank the commenter who you got your idea from.

5. Do a Q&A or an AMA (Ask Me Anything) in the comments section. Your subscribers or viewers are interested to get to know the person behind the channel. So open yourself up to your audience and they will appreciate you more for it. Alternatively, you can gather all the questions in the comments section and shoot a video of yourself answering it—another new material you can work on coming from the comments your viewers made.

6. Do not engage in heated debates. It's just not worth your time. Furthermore, never troll or flame commenters. You want to be seen as a professional so leave the comments PG. Know that you can never please everyone. There will always be haters out there. Learn how to ignore them if all they send is hate. But if they have something substantial to say and you can use it for your development, take their criticism and swallow your pride. You will be better off because of it.

Go ahead and start engaging with your subscribers. This part should be the easiest to do. All it takes is for you to just be yourself. Approach your interaction with an open mind and you will come out better for it. And acknowledge that you don't have a monopoly on great ideas. As you interact, your subscribers will trust you more and may even share their brilliant ideas with you. That right there is a goldmine.

Conclusions

As you reach the end you will realize that creating a YouTube channel is not that difficult. The real challenge comes once you already have an existing channel to maintain. If you follow the steps outlined here you will definitely see a steady increase in your subscriber count. The keys to making your YouTube Channel a success are:

- **Deep knowledge** of your audience base. If you know who you are making your videos for it should be easy to come out with relevant content that is both useful and fun.

- **Play around** with different types of content. If you are an educational channel, don't bore your subscribers with just tutorial videos. You can actually mix things up by coming up with different types of videos. Why not pair tutorials with product or service reviews and even comedy skits and (think memes) and performance videos.

- **Take advantage** of YouTube's analytics capabilities and see what types of videos bring engagement. The data will bring insights on what content you should be focusing on. Don't just live with one data set. Try to mix and match data sets to come up with stronger analyses.

- **Create an even bigger** ecosystem where your subscribers can further interact with you. Link your YouTube Channel with your web page and social media pages. In doing so, not only will you create more interaction, you can also reach a wider and more targeted audience base.

- **Lastly**, bring out the human side of your channel and start interacting with your commenters. People appreciate brands and channels who take the time to interact with their users. Interacting gives you the chance to get to know more about your subscribers (which will give you a deeper knowledge of their needs and wants), give you feedback for improvement, and can also generate ideas for material you can use as content in the future.

To end, make sure you are having fun and enjoying the whole process. This should be the whole unifying theme of your YouTube Channel. Creating your channel and managing it allows you to create something oft value to others. As a result, it touches others' being as they resonate with your content. Be an artist and a brand ambassador all at the same time. Create with passion and expose your soul in the process. At the end of the day, it's not the number of views or the subscriber count that matters. It's the joy and satisfaction you get in running your very own YouTube Channel.

9 798456 529190